SEEN:
HOPE AND HEALING
FOR SINGLE MOMS

MICHELLE DONNELLY

Published by Agape Moms LLC Copyright © 2019 Michelle Donnelly

ISBN: 978-1-7333839-0-5

Learn more about Agape Moms at www.agapemoms.com

DEDICATION

For my precious arrows– Sissy, Bubba, and CiCi.

Children are a gift from the LORD;
  they are a reward from him.
Children born to a young man
  are like arrows in a warrior's hands.
How joyful is the man whose quiver is full of them!
  He will not be put to shame when he confronts his accusers at the city gates.

Psalm 127: 3-5

Contents

Introduction: The God Who Sees

Okay girl, let's get real. As a single mom, I know you've felt forgotten about. Overlooked. Maybe even shamed. You may have been told that being a single mom marks you as a failure.

And worse yet, you may have even believed it.

But what if I told you that God has a special place in His heart, specifically for single women? And I'm not just talking about the righteous Ruths of the Bible who may have lost their husbands to untimely death (though if that's you, you are ABSOLUTELY included). I'm also talking about your average cast-off, rejected, goodbye-and-good-riddance single mom.

Let me introduce you to one such woman from the book of Genesis. Her name was Hagar. Hagar was an Egyptian servant of Sarai, the wife of Abram (if those names sound unfamiliar, Sarai and Abram later became known as Sarah and Abraham).

Abram and Sarai were getting up there in years (we are talking OLD) and hadn't yet been able to have any kids of their own. Despite her age, Sarai's biological clock was still tick-tick-ticking. Eventually, Sarai figures if she can't bear a child, maybe she'll be better off raising someone else's baby as her own. Taking matters into her own hands, Sarai decides Abram should take Hagar as a wife, that Hagar might conceive an heir for Sarai and Abram to raise.

I'm sure you can see where this is going. The Bible really is better than reality TV.

As soon as Hagar becomes pregnant, things get dicey between the two women. Hagar starts taunting Sarai, flaunting her fertility in the face of the barren old woman. Sarai tries to get Abram to do something about it, but he kind of tells her it's up to her to handle it. Well, Sarai chooses the "Mean Girls" route and manages the situation via retaliation. Sarai torments Hagar so badly that Hagar flees to the wilderness to escape the mistreatment. Lonely and afraid, Hagar sits beside a well and weeps.

Suddenly, the Angel of the Lord appears to Hagar. He explains that Hagar should go back to Abram and Sarai, but that God's not sending her empty-handed. He delivers this promise– Hagar will be blessed with more descendants than she can count. Furthermore, the Angel of the Lord instructs Hagar to name her unborn child Ishmael, which means "God hears." He tells Hagar to do this so she will have a constant reminder of this incredible moment, when God heard and answered her desperate cries.

As you can imagine, Hagar was beyond amazed. Here she was pregnant– running for her life– and in a moment of great desperation, she was personally comforted by God. On top of that, Hagar received special, specific blessings.

Validation. Reassurance. Promise.

After this visitation, Hagar realized that God had a specific calling and purpose for her life. She knew, without a doubt, that God saw her– not as a cast-off woman, but as a treasured daughter.

After this encounter, Hagar began referring to God by a special name, "El Roi."

In Hebrew, El Roi means "the God who sees me."

(Sweet mama, I know you know as a single mother how glorious it is to be seen. Does our God know us or what?!).

After all of this, I bet Hagar probably thought her relationships with Sarai and Abram (now called Sarah and Abraham) would be easy-peasy-lemon-squeezy. They weren't. Hagar returns home and gives birth to Ishmael. However, several years later, God promises to give Sarah and Abraham an heir of their own, and a very elderly Sarah gives birth to Isaac.

As Ishmael and Isaac grow, a little sibling rivalry sets in and Ishmael begins teasing his new little brother. Finally, Sarah can't take it anymore (raise your hand if you've been there) and asks Abraham to send Hagar and Ishmael away, for good.

Of course, Abraham is troubled by this. But God assures Abraham that if he sends them away, He will care for them. So Abraham rises early one morning, packs up a little food and water, and sends Hagar and Ishmael into the wilderness.

Now homeless, Hagar and Ishmael aimlessly wander the desert. Once the water runs out, Hagar is certain she is going to have to watch her only son die, right in front of her. She must have thought, "What good are all those promises from God if we die right here!"

But God wasn't done yet.

Above Ishmael's feeble whimpers, the Angel of God calls down to Hagar from Heaven. He says, "Hagar, what's wrong? Do not be afraid! God has heard the boy crying as he lies there." In this moment, Hagar is ever-so-gently reminded that the God who comforted her when she first cried out as a pregnant refugee still sees her and that the promises He made to her are still good.

Suddenly, God opens Hagar's eyes to reveal a fresh spring of water nearby. Hagar quickly revives Ishmael with a drink from the spring, and the pair continues on their way. Years pass, and under God's watchful care, Ishmael grows into a strong and skillful young man with many descendants, just as Hagar had been promised.

Hagar wasn't perfect. She'd made some mistakes along the way. But God saw Hagar's suffering. God knew her pain. And even when she had forgotten all that God had promised her, God didn't abandon her. He didn't take His promises away. He comforted her. He reassured her. He reminded her how valuable she was to Him. And every time Hagar got knocked down, God was there, making a way.

Sister, this isn't just a Bible story about some woman in the distant past. Hagar's story is a revelation of God's lovingkindness and compassion toward all of us– and it's for you too.

You are seen. You are loved. And God has great plans for you. Whatever you're going through, it is not the end. God's writing a whole new chapter in a beautiful story. Through the course of this study, you're going to discover God's incredible promises for your life. But better yet, like Hagar, I pray you will experience God's comforting presence and healing power, that you would step into the light of the new life He has for you.

You can read the complete story of Hagar in the Book of Genesis, specifically chapters 16 and 21.

How to Use this Book

Each chapter in this study features five distinct sections to guide you on your journey toward healing and hope: PROBLEM, PASSAGE, PROMISES, PLAN, & PRAYER.

PROBLEM

"Give all your worries and cares to God, for he cares about you."

1 Peter 5:7

Life can be really overwhelming. God knows this, and He invites us to give our burdens and stresses to Him. But sometimes, we don't really understand what's bothering us in the first place! At the beginning of each chapter, you'll have the opportunity to identify a specific PROBLEM you're dealing with that relates to the topic covered in that chapter. Once you've written down your answer, spend a moment in prayer asking God to help you remove any emotional or spiritual barriers you are experiencing with this problem, so you can see how He wants you to move forward. Knowing what you're struggling with, and giving it to the Lord, will help you gain clarity as you move through the rest of the chapter.

PASSAGE

"All Scripture is inspired by God and is useful to teach us what is true and to make us realize what is wrong in our lives. It corrects us when we are wrong and teaches us to do what is right."

2 Timothy 3:16

I laugh when people say, "There's no instruction manual for life." They're wrong. The Bible contains God's wisdom and promises for us, and it's useful for any and every stage of our lives. It's a divine love letter, given to us by a doting Father who wants us to know His goodness– for real. In each chapter, you'll find a specific PASSAGE of Scripture selected to guide your understanding of the topic being addressed. Unless otherwise specified, each passage is taken from the New Living Translation of the Bible (NLT). There are other fantastic translations that you may also enjoy referencing, but for our purposes, the NLT is well suited for both first-time-readers and long-time-lovers of the Bible alike.

PROMISES

"The LORD says, "I will guide you along the best pathway for your life. I will advise you and watch over you."

Psalm 32:8

Reading the Bible is one thing. But *studying* the Bible– that's the good stuff. Really digging into God's Word gives us the ability to perceive His perfect will and gracious promises for our lives, through the power of the Holy Spirit. The PROMISES section features study questions designed to help you discover what God has planned for you, both in this season of your life and beyond. And it's okay if as you read you see things a little differently or if you have doubts or questions. God wants you to bring those to Him in prayer so He can show you the answers!

PLAN

"Anyone who listens to my teaching and follows it is wise, like a person who builds a house on solid rock."

Matthew 7:24

This isn't a warm-and-fuzzy kind of Bible study. God is in the business of changing lives, and understanding His promises will reveal what we need to do to walk in them. Sometimes, we may be called to change things up and try something new. Sometimes, we need to clear away old baggage and bad habits that are dragging us down. Either way, the PLAN section offers you the opportunity to reflect on the promises you've discovered in the selected passage, and discern what you need to do to walk in them. Change is something best done in stages, so don't feel the need to adjust everything all at once. Prayerfully consider even a single step you know you can follow through on, and believe that with the empowering of the Holy Spirit, your transformation will begin.

PRAYER

"And we are confident that he hears us whenever we ask for anything that pleases him."

1 John 5:14

Prayer is precious. Think about it, it's our open line to talk with the God of the Universe– anytime, anywhere! And He wants to hear all of it. Our problems. Our pain. Our plans. Our petitions. At the conclusion of each section, you'll find a PRAYER intended to help guide your conversation with God about the topic that was covered. You'll also find some blank space to add your own requests and/ or pray about the next steps you just identified in that chapter's PLAN section. Allow this time of prayer to be a starting point to an ongoing conversation with God about your healing process, as you continue to seek to understand His promises and plan for you.

SEEN:
HOPE AND HEALING
FOR SINGLE MOMS

BIBLE STUDY LESSONS

1
Discovering God's Promises for Your Life

Circumstances in our lives can make us feel like we've missed out on God's best. When we look at the ashes of the life we thought we'd have, we may wonder if God even sees us. We may be confused, wondering why things have ended up the way they have. We may even feel so guilty about what's happened in the past that we doubt we'll ever really be good enough to receive God's love and promises at all.

Sweet sister, I've been there too. You are so not alone.

Funny thing is, God actually knows these things are on our minds, yet we're the ones suffering because we think we can't talk to Him about it. The truth is, God sees your pain, and He wants you to bring it all to Him– the good, the bad, and the really, really bad– so He can *set you free*.

Psalm 40:5 says that God's plans for us are "too many to list!" It's okay if you don't see that yet. The first step is claiming the victory Jesus has already won over your suffering as your own. Like really own it. Believe it. Trust it is already yours.

In this section, you're going to uncover the promises God has for you, and identify what is holding you back from walking in His peace and freedom in your life today.

PROBLEM

How have you struggled with believing God sees you, loves you, and has good things for you?

PASSAGE

> 3 By his divine power, God has given us everything we need for living a godly life. We have received all of this by coming to know him, the one who called us to himself by means of his marvelous glory and excellence. 4 And because of his glory and excellence, he has given us great and precious promises. These are the promises that enable you to share his divine nature and escape the world's corruption caused by human desires.
>
> 5 In view of all this, make every effort to respond to God's promises. Supplement your faith with a generous provision of moral excellence, and moral excellence with knowledge, 6 and knowledge with self-control, and self-control with patient endurance, and patient endurance with godliness, 7 and godliness with brotherly affection, and brotherly affection with love for everyone.
>
> 8 The more you grow like this, the more productive and useful you will be in your knowledge of our Lord Jesus Christ. 9 But those who fail to develop in this way are shortsighted or blind, forgetting that they have been cleansed from their old sins.
>
> 10 So, dear brothers and sisters, work hard to prove that you really are among those God has called and chosen. Do these things, and you will never fall away. 11 Then God will give you a grand entrance into the eternal Kingdom of our Lord and Savior Jesus Christ.
>
> 2 Peter 1:3-11

PROMISES

How do we come to know God and receive His power and promises (verse 3)? Underline the words that support your answer.

Circle the words in verse 3 that show why God has chosen to give us His love and promises. How does this evidence refute the idea that we have to earn the things God has for us?

Circle the words that describe God's promises for those He has called. For what two reasons does verse 4 tell us God wants us to have these things?

1.

2.

These two gifts give us freedom, not only in eternity but also from the troubles of our lives <u>today</u>. This passage tells us God helps us "escape" the corruption that keeps us from experiencing His freedom. What wrong thoughts or actions keep you feeling bound up in chains?

While God's gifts for us do not have to be earned, verse 5 tells us that we have a choice to respond and accept God's promises. What has kept you from accepting that God has promised good things for you?

When it comes to what we really believe, our actions speak louder than our words. Verses 5-7 tell us that growing in faith is the way we show that we accept God's promises for us. List the 7 ways these verses encourage us to open ourselves to God's love.

1.

2.

3.

4.

5.

6.

7.

How do you think each area leads you to the next one, allowing you to walk in greater freedom as you grow?

Verse 8 promises us that growing in these areas will give us the freedom to discover our purpose in life. Underline the words that provide evidence for this. Where does verse 8 say our purpose is ultimately rooted?

Jesus knew you needed freedom before you ever knew you were trapped. In His great love for you, He died to set you free, so you could drop all your old baggage and discover your life's purpose. But verse 9 tells us if we don't choose to walk in that truth, there's one major promise we've forgotten– what is it?

Do you ever feel like you've forgotten this? How has this affected your ability to discover His promises and purposes for your life?

In verse 10, what two words describe God's view of you?

1.

2.

Called. Chosen. Girl, you are valuable! God has great things for you to do, and Jesus's death and resurrection have already unchained you from your sin and the pain of your past. God wants you to walk in His victory, <u>certain</u> of the fantastic future He has for you.

What does verse 11 say is the ultimate promise God wants to give all of us?

Circle the words that describe the type of feeling we will experience when we receive this great reward. What kind of feeling do these words give you, especially when you consider where you are at in life right now?

Now that you have read the truth of God's unconditional love and promises for those He's called, what doubts have you had that this is true for you?

What influences and choices in your life, past and present, have allowed corruption to sneak in to rob you of peace and freedom?

Verse 4 tells us that God wants to help us escape from the corruption in the world that destroys our ability to walk in the love and freedom Jesus has already given us. What bad influences, habits, thoughts, or distractions do you need to get away from so you can start experiencing His peace?

What is something you can do this week to start clearing these things out of your life?

How do you think you'll feel when you allow God to help you conquer what's holding you back so you can experience complete freedom?

PRAYER

Loving Father, thank you for the love you want to give to me, free of charge. Your Word tells me that you want to bless me with great and precious promises– promises to set me free from the darkness in this world that keeps me away from the love and peace you have for me. These promises aren't just for other people, Lord– you say they are for me. Sometimes, I feel weak and I have a hard time believing that. Help me to accept your love and promises, God. Help me to live that out by growing closer to you, and rejecting the things that hold me back. Give me the strength this week to get away from things that have been robbing me of the peace you have for me.

_____

_____

_____

I want to walk in your peace and victory, Father. Thank you for loving me and gently showing me the way. In Jesus's name, I pray. Amen.

2
Recovering Your Worth

I remember the first time I was invited to join a group for single mothers. The group leader had approached me and asked me to come and check it out. I hated the idea. I felt so labeled, so deficient, being called a "single mom." Not only did I feel like being identified as a single mom made me a failure (yuck), but it also forced me to relive the painful reality of my circumstances every time I heard it (double yuck).

Because of all the hang-ups I had with being identified as a single mom, I decided it would just be easier to avoid the whole thing so I didn't have to feel so labeled (no scarlet letter for me, thank you). Of course, I came up with some totally lame excuse to get out of going to the group. After blowing off the invitation, I thought, "Whew! Now the group leader will realize I just can't add one more thing to my life. Surely she'll take the hint and leave me alone."

But the sweet woman who ran the group persisted and invited me again. Knowing I couldn't avoid her forever, I figured I should be polite and go at least once. Before I even walked into that first meeting, I was already armed with a list of excuses as to why I wouldn't be able to come back. That it was too hard for me to fit it into my schedule. That it just wasn't for me.

But God didn't let me get away that easily. He broke me down that first night, showing me that all the negative associations I'd had with being labeled a single mom were lies of the Enemy, meant to hold me back from what God had for me. He showed me that while single motherhood is a reality of my situation, it's not a definition of who I am.

And now here I am, neck-deep in single mothers' ministry and *loving it*. God is funny like that.

But I shouldn't be surprised– when we accept the identity we have in Christ, the purpose of our lives (and our pain) becomes so clear. Romans 8:28 says that "God causes everything to work together for the good of those who love God and are called according to his purpose for them." Being a single mom doesn't define you, but it does give you a unique opportunity to bless and be blessed if *you choose* to let God use it for good.

In this section, you're going to discover how God sees you, who He says you are in His sight. You'll also explore the beautiful plans He has for your life, things He planned for you well before you ever drew your first breath.

PROBLEM

Discuss how being labeled a "single mom" has impacted you negatively.

PASSAGE

> 4 But God is so rich in mercy, and he loved us so much, 5 that even though we were dead because of our sins, he gave us life when he raised Christ from the dead. (It is only by God's grace that you have been saved!) 6 For he raised us from the dead along with Christ and seated us with him in the heavenly realms because we are united with Christ Jesus. 7 So God can point to us in all future ages as examples of the incredible wealth of his grace and kindness toward us, as shown in all he has done for us who are united with Christ Jesus.
>
> 8 God saved you by his grace when you believed. And you can't take credit for this; it is a gift from God. 9 Salvation is not a reward for the good things we have done, so none of us can boast about it. 10 For we are God's masterpiece. He has created us anew in Christ Jesus, so we can do the good things he planned for us long ago.
>
> Ephesians 2:4-10

PROMISES

What gifts did God give us when he raised Jesus from the dead? Circle the words in verse 5 that support your answer.

Underline the words that show what state we were in when God decided to give us these gifts.

That could have been the end of the story right there. But God doesn't allow us to be defined by sin and failure. Go back to verse 4– why would God do all of this for us?

> Because God loves us, that means we should really think of ourselves as
> *being loved* – beloved.

Verse 6 tells us where God seats us when we accept Jesus Christ as our Lord and Savior. Where is it? Underline the words that support your answer.

Underline the reason verse 6 tells us we can be seated with Christ. Do you feel this describes your connection to Him right now? Why or why not?

When verse 6 tells us we are united with Christ, it's not only describing our relationship with Him; it's talking about who we become in the very core of our nature. Being joined to Jesus means being transformed by His love and power into the kind of women the world has no authority to define. *This* is how God sees us, and how we should see ourselves.

Knowing (without a doubt!) that in the eyes of Jesus you are worth dying for– worth *saving*– regardless of your weaknesses and failures, empowers you to reject all the lies you've ever believed about yourself.

How does this truth change the way you have been viewing yourself and the source of your value?

What does verse 7 tell us we receive when we choose to be identified with Christ? How does this differ from what we experience when we allow things of this world to define us?

Sometimes it seems too good to be true– that when it comes to God's love and promises, we just can't measure up. What do verses 8 & 9 say about that?

Underline the word in verse 10 that describes how God views you in Christ (and how you should view yourself when you commit your life to Him). Think of the qualities that make something a masterpiece and list them here.

How do you feel when you realize this is who God says you are in Christ?

This passage closes with a reminder that your identity in Christ also gives you *purpose* as you embrace how God sees you to become the woman He designed you to be. What does verse 10 say God has planned for you in your life?

When does it say God planned these things?

PLAN

How does this passage change the way you understand how God sees you?

How do you need to change the way you see yourself to align with how God views you?

What lies, about God or yourself, do you need to stop believing?

What thoughts, activities, objects, or people are giving you a false sense of worth right now?

What is something you can change this week to move away from those things, to establish your value in Christ instead?

When it comes to the "future ages" God has chosen for you to influence (verse 7), who specifically comes to mind?

How would you like to grow in your influence of them?

Who is someone you know that can mentor you and help you stay focused on finding your value in your relationship with Jesus? When can you contact them to meet with them this week?

To further root your identity in Christ, do you still need to accept Him as your Lord and Savior, or make a fresh commitment to follow Him? If so, add this to your prayer to close out this chapter.

PRAYER

Lord God, thank you for making me your masterpiece. Even when I haven't always felt that way about myself, you have gently led me to your Word that tells me the truth about how much you love me and how lovely your thoughts are towards me. Forgive me for believing lies that have caused me to think wrongly about myself. Give me the faith to believe what you say, so I can fully know how it feels to be united with Christ and become the woman you made me to be. Help me to experience this unity so completely, that it gives me the excitement and the courage to bless others around me with your love.

_____

_____

_____

_____

Thank you for your gift of grace that makes all of this possible, Father. Thank you for choosing me to receive this gift, which I could never earn on my own. How great your love is for me! In the name of Jesus, I pray. Amen.

3
Finally Free: Life Without Shame and Regret

What if? If only? I know these thoughts have probably consumed you at some point in the not-so-distant past. To cope with the pain of our current circumstances, we often end up examining the things of the past, wondering what could have been had life gone a little differently.

But my dear, spending too much time in the past is a trap (after all, you're not even going that way).

Now don't get me wrong, I know a wise woman learns from her past. She uses it to understand her situation and make adjustments where possible. But she does all this with the intention of moving *forward*, rather than letting shame, disappointment, and regret hold her back.

Ecclesiastes 7:10 says, "Don't long for 'the good old days.' This is not wise." If we're being honest, for many of us, the good old days may not have actually been all that good. But in comparison, we might feel like they were at least better than what we're dealing with right now!

But God's way looks forward, not backward. The promises of God are meant to teach us to *expect* God will do great things with the broken pieces of our lives. It looks at what can be (what will be!), rather than what was (or wasn't).

2 Corinthians 5:17 tells us that when we are in Christ, each of us becomes a new person– that "the old life is gone; a new life has begun!" Jesus conquered the shame of your past with His death and resurrection, so you can live free of it and move into His glorious future.

And that's the way you're headed, sister.

This liberated life is now yours for the taking; but actually walking in all that freedom, that's a choice. Some of the things that keep us bound in shame are not our fault. Some of them are. Either way, Christ has secured victory over *all of it*. The bars to your own personal prison have been flung wide open. But it's up to you– are you going to stay put? Or are you going to follow His lead and get out of there?

In this section, you will have a look at the way God views your weaknesses, so you can reshape your thinking about the disappointments that may still be holding you back. We'll also discuss the importance of making the choice to turn from sin and shame to walk freely in God's love and compassion.

PROBLEM

What shame do you feel with regard to yourself, your life, and your past?

PASSAGE

> 8 The LORD is compassionate and merciful,
> slow to get angry and filled with unfailing love.
>
> 9 He will not constantly accuse us,
> nor remain angry forever.
>
> 10 He does not punish us for all our sins;
> he does not deal harshly with us, as we deserve.
>
> 11 For his unfailing love toward those who fear him
> is as great as the height of the heavens above the earth.
>
> 12 He has removed our sins as far from us
> as the east is from the west.
>
> 13 The LORD is like a father to his children,
> tender and compassionate to those who fear him.
>
> 14 For he knows how weak we are;
> he remembers we are only dust.
>
> 15 Our days on earth are like grass;
> like wildflowers, we bloom and die.
>
> 16 The wind blows, and we are gone—
> as though we had never been here.
>
> 17 But the love of the LORD remains forever
> with those who fear him.
> His salvation extends to the children's children
>
> 18 of those who are faithful to his covenant,
> of those who obey his commandments!
>
> Psalm 103:8-18

PROMISES

We'll start our study of this passage by personalizing this text. Every time you see the words "we" or "us," cross them out and insert your own name. How does it make you feel to see the thoughts and actions of God positioned towards you specifically, rather than the usual "we" that's seen in the Bible?

In verses 9 and 10, circle every time you see the word "not" or "nor." Now underline each action that the text says God does not do. How do these phrases help you understand how God views the disappointing parts of your past?

Verses 11 and 12 describe the lengths God's love goes to remove sin and shame from us. How do these examples help you understand the distance God has put between you and your sin through the death and resurrection of Jesus?

Circle the words in verse 13 that describe God's relationship to us. When you consider your own life experience, does this word picture help or hurt your understanding of God?

Verse 13 lists just two of the many characteristics that make God a *perfect* Father – what are they?

Underline what verse 14 says God knows about us. How does this help you understand how God views your weaknesses and failures, both past and present?

What keeps you from viewing yourself this way?

What do verses 15 and 16 show you about human life?

How does verse 17 show God's love differs from the limitations of human life? Underline the word or words that support your answer. How does it make you feel to know this difference between God and mankind exists?

Look at verses 17 and 18. What do these verses mean to you as a mother? How do they help you understand the promises God has for your children?

Whom do verses 11,13, and 17 say God's tenderness and compassion is available to?

Deeply reflecting on all God's power, goodness, and generosity inspires the kind of awe and humility that drives us to honor and follow Him; that's a good way to understand fear of the Lord. Verse 18 shows that our fear of the Lord is on display in our lives when we choose to turn away from sin, shame, and unforgiveness.

It's then that we experience the true peace of walking in His grace.

Knowing this, where can you grow in turning away from shame and regret so you can more fully experience the mercy and compassion God has for you?

PLAN

How has your understanding of the Passage reshaped the way you believe you should view your past and your weaknesses?

How is this different from the way you have previously viewed yourself and your life?

This Passage is clear that the Lord's compassion is available to anyone who fears Him. How does it make you feel to know He offers you His compassion, even <u>before</u> you make a choice to follow Him?

Pain from the past often keeps us from experiencing God's healing for us in the present. When we turn to things other than God to cope with pain, we may feel comforted– but only temporarily. What recurring pain are you struggling with in your life?

Memorizing Scripture is a great way to allow God's truth to not only encourage us but also retrain our thoughts. Write down a verse from this week's Passage that you can pray whenever you feel disappointed, ashamed, or regretful.

Over the next week, chose a time each day to commit the verse you have chosen to memory. Write the time you have selected here.

Do you feel you need any additional mentoring, counseling, or support to help you with changing your perspective on yourself and your past so you can walk in freedom? Do your children?

If so, plan out who you need to speak to this week and write down when you will do it below.

PRAYER

Loving Father, you know that I have felt shame and disappointment about things in my life, about myself. I am thankful, Father, that you don't hold my weaknesses against me and that you have cast my sin as far as the east is from the west, so I can be free from the guilt of it all. Free to follow you. I need your help, Lord, with seeing myself and my life the way you see it. I need help with removing the pain from my life, so I can continue to grow in your love and guide my children in doing the same.

_____

_____

_____

_____

I know, God, that you don't want to see me held back by things I can't change. With your guidance, Father, I know I can learn from these experiences, and find peace in your tenderness and compassion towards me. I ask for your strength and wisdom as I move forward, so I can leave behind sin and pain and walk in your love and freedom. In the name of Jesus, I pray. Amen.

4

Forgiving Others (Even When They're Not Sorry)

We've all had to deal with the consequences of choices we didn't make. If you think about it, it's because of choices we didn't make that each of us has life in the first place!

But sometimes, we have to deal with the consequences of another person's poor decisions, decisions that really aren't so life-giving. In fact, I know some of us might even say the fallout has been life-robbing (I'm only saying it because you're thinking it).

While living with the consequences of someone else's choices may feel bad, unforgiveness is worse. Have you ever heard the expression that "choosing not to forgive is like drinking poison and hoping the other person will die?" Well, it's not in the Bible, but it echoes the teachings of Hebrews 12:15, that we should "watch out that no poisonous root of bitterness grows up to trouble you, corrupting many."

Corrupting *many*. The poison of unforgiveness doesn't just harm us, it harms those around us (including our kiddos).

But forgiveness isn't just for the good of others; it's intended to free us from the influences of evil that come along with holding a grudge. In 2 Corinthians 2:10-11, Paul tells us that forgiveness is for our benefit, so "that Satan will not outsmart us...[because] we are familiar with his evil schemes." Simply put, when we don't forgive, we are falling for Satan's trickery.

And I'll tell you what, sugar. We're too smart for that.

In this section, you'll learn about the steps toward complete forgiveness (even for those who have hurt you but may be kinda "sorry, not sorry" about it). You'll also learn about how to interact with those you've forgiven, even when they reject your efforts to make peace.

PROBLEM

Who do you have a hard time forgiving? Why?

PASSAGE

14 Bless those who persecute you. Don't curse them; pray that God will bless them. 15 Be happy with those who are happy, and weep with those who weep. 16 Live in harmony with each other. Don't be too proud to enjoy the company of ordinary people. And don't think you know it all!

17 Never pay back evil with more evil. Do things in such a way that everyone can see you are honorable. 18 Do all that you can to live in peace with everyone.

19 Dear friends, never take revenge. Leave that to the righteous anger of God. For the Scriptures say,

"I will take revenge; I will pay them back," says the LORD.

20 Instead, "If your enemies are hungry, feed them. If they are thirsty, give them something to drink. In doing this, you will heap burning coals of shame on their heads."

21 Don't let evil conquer you, but conquer evil by doing good.

Romans 12:14-21

PROMISES

Verse 14 tells us how to start the process of forgiveness. What does this verse say we should do to get our hearts oriented correctly towards those who have hurt us?

Does this seem like an impossible task right now when you think about those who have hurt you?

How does verse 15 say we should react when we learn that anyone, even a person who has hurt us, receives good news? Bad news?

How does verse 16 say we should seek to relate to others, in our own thoughts and behaviors?

The next three sentences describe the ways in which we, in and of ourselves, make living in harmony difficult. What are they?

1.

2.

3.

How is unforgiveness a factor in these three areas?

What does verse 17 say is the goal of all our interactions with others?

Verse 18 helps us to understand that not all relationships will be ideal. It tells to what extent we have the responsibility to foster peace with others.

Does verse 18 suggest there may be a limitation on complete reconciliation and restoration in human relationships? Underline the words that support your answer. Add any additional thoughts you have on this below.

We can't force others to respond to us in a peaceful manner. And while we are still called to forgiveness, *trusting* a person who continues to injure us is a separate matter.

How does this understanding help you grasp the importance of appropriate boundaries with individuals who reject our efforts to create peace?

Underline the words in verse 19 that show how God will deal with wrongdoing. How does this make you feel when you think about those who have hurt you?

How does it make you feel when you think about how you've treated others?

When you look at this verse, does forgiveness excuse what others have done?

> Despite how others treat us, verse 19 teaches us not to take matters into our own hands by retaliating.

God's judgment should be both vindicating AND humbling. In light of that, how does verse 20 say we should treat our enemies?

Do you think you can do this in the way God desires if you have any unforgiveness towards them?

What does it mean when the text says "you will heap burning coals of shame on their heads?" What kind of results should our good deeds have?

Circle the word in verse 21 that describes our position as it relates to evil when we do good. Why do you think it's important to pursue this?

PLAN

How will forgiving those who have hurt you set you free?

When considering those who have hurt you, how do you need to change your thoughts and attitude to align yourself with the guidance of this Passage?

How could your prayers better reflect what this Passage teaches?

What revenge have you been enacting on those who have hurt you?

How has unforgiveness affected your ability to experience peace on a daily basis?

Has it affected your children? In what ways?

What is one thing you can do this week to move forward in the process of forgiving others?

PRAYER

Lord, I am so thankful for your gift of forgiveness. You have shown me in your Word that you forgave me of all my wrongdoing against you, even when I didn't deserve it. But when I look at those who have hurt me, Lord, it is hard to forgive them, especially when they aren't sorry. But I know unforgiveness is a trap you want to liberate me from so I can live in peace. I need your help to even want to forgive in the first place, Lord.

_____

_____

_____

_____

Father, help me trust that your way of handling these relationships is better than mine. Please give me your wisdom so I may know how to use appropriate boundaries to guard the peace that forgiveness puts in my heart. In the name of Jesus, I pray. Amen.

Overcoming Doubt and Discouragement

God's Word tells us more than just who God says we are— it declares *who He is*. Much of the doubt we experience in trusting God and His promises comes from the fear that He will turn away from us or let us down, like so many people in the past have.

Let's be honest – we've all been afraid that maybe God's just not going to show up.

But Numbers 23:19 says, "God is not a man, so He does not lie. God is not human, so He does not change His mind. Has He ever spoken and failed to act? Has He ever promised and not carried it through?"

(BTW, the answer to those last two questions is NO).

And even when we do believe God will come through, we still may not totally get what He's doing (or why it's taking so long). It's easy to get discouraged when we're in the dark. But 1 John 1:5 reminds us "God is light, and there is no darkness in Him at all." We can trust that God's methods are <u>always</u> good, even when we don't understand how it's all going to play out.

What fills in the gap between the known and unknown is faith.

Faith in the midst of uncertainty allows us to completely rely on God, without anxiety or distress. God desires that we would find rest in the fact that He is the ultimate Protector and Provider, which is why Isaiah 54:5 says, "your Creator will be your Husband."

Now let's be real here for a minute – I know for some, that word picture doesn't conjure up the best feeling. Your previous relationships may have distorted this imagery a bit. But we can find comfort in the fact that God created marriage, and He knows how to be a husband in the most *perfect* way. He's a husband who knows what's good for us and draws us closer to Him, so He can lavish His extravagant love on us.

But doubt tries to confuse us in an effort to snatch these promises from us. It makes us think of God in human terms, with the same limitations of those who have claimed to love us before. But God is not a husband who abandons. Not a husband who hurts. Not a husband who dies. Not a husband who abuses for selfish gain.

The antidote to the poison of our doubt is the belief that God is who <u>He says He is</u>, a realization we can come to only through His gift of faith.

In this section, you will see what true faith is, and the power it gives believers to overcome uncertainty. You will also start to understand the role of faith in enhancing your ability to trust God, even when you don't understand His plan.

PROBLEM

How does doubt keep you from believing God still wants to do incredible things in your life?

PASSAGE

> 1 Faith is the confidence that what we hope for will actually happen; it gives us assurance about things we cannot see. 2 Through their faith, the people in days of old earned a good reputation.
>
> 3 By faith we understand that the entire universe was formed at God's command, that what we now see did not come from anything that can be seen.
>
> 4 It was by faith that Abel brought a more acceptable offering to God than Cain did. Abel's offering gave evidence that he was a righteous man, and God showed his approval of his gifts. Although Abel is long dead, he still speaks to us by his example of faith.
>
> 5 It was by faith that Enoch was taken up to heaven without dying—"he disappeared, because God took him." For before he was taken up, he was known as a person who pleased God. 6 And it is impossible to please God without faith. Anyone who wants to come to him must believe that God exists and that he rewards those who sincerely seek him.
>
> Hebrews 11:1-6

PROMISES

Underline what verse 1 says faith is. What does verse 1 say true faith gives us?

How do you think it would feel to experience complete assurance, despite difficult circumstances?

Oftentimes, we substitute the word "hope" with the word "wish" (as in, "I *hope* someday I will come home to a clean house").

But that's not how the Bible uses the word "hope."

How does verse 1 show us that hope in God is so much more than a wish?

In what aspects of your life do you struggle to have this kind of hope?

Verse 2 says there's an additional benefit of faith. What is it?

Knowing our time on Earth is limited, why do you think a reputation of faith matters?

> When we are long gone, a reputation of faith is a legacy, a beacon of light, we can leave to our loved ones, just like the "people of old."
>
> More on them in a minute.

Verse 3 tells us in order to believe God created the entire universe, we have to have something specific. What is it?

While faith allows us to know *that* God created the universe, that does NOT mean we understand *how* or *why* He did it. How does this correlate with the things in your own life that you don't have answers for?

Remember those faith-filled "people of old" referenced back in verse 2? We're about to meet a couple of them. We'll start with Abel. Why does verse 4 say Abel was able to bring a "more acceptable" offering to God?

What does verse 4 say Abel's faith in action demonstrated about him? How did God respond to this faith?

Now there's Enoch. Why was he able to be "taken up to heaven without dying"?

What was Enoch's reputation, even before he was taken up?

Considering these verses about Abel and Enoch, what do you think this Passage reveals about the relationship between faith and actions?

But a box around the word "faith," each time it occurs in relation to Abel or Enoch. How many times did you box this word? Why do you think it is used so often?

The frequency with which the words "by faith" are used shows that these guys were **not** superheroes all on their own. They were not great because of anything *they did* apart from God; they were great because of the things *God did* through them, because of their faith in God and the goodness of His plan.

What does this show you faith can open you up to?

Can we please God just by doing good deeds on our own, without faith? Write down the words in verse 6 that prove your answer.

In contrast, what two things does verse 6 say will actually lead us to fully experiencing closeness with God?

    1.

    2.

How do you struggle in these two areas?

How have people or experiences in your past distorted your view of who God is?

Over the last several weeks we've been studying God's character and promises. How has what you've studied corrected your view of God?

Now we know from this Passage that deep faith gives us assurance. What is still keeping you from having full assurance that God's promises "will actually happen" for you?

What does the Word say about that?

What triggers of fear and doubt do you regularly experience?

When faced with doubt, fear, and stress, how do you typically respond?

Do you think the way you respond currently is helping you grow and thrive in your relationship with God? Why or why not?

External coping mechanisms or "crutches" tend to keep us in a cycle of fear. But turning to God and embracing His promises grows our faith to set us free from fear. When faced with negative thoughts or emotions this week, what strategies can you use to turn from your usual "crutches" to a dependency on God instead?

How can you involve your mentor to help you follow through with implementing these new strategies?

Father God, how incredible it is that you made the entire universe, and yet you also have unique plans just for me. God, sometimes I have trouble believing this; I have trouble understanding why you do things the way you do. I see that I need faith to believe what you say and allow your promises to sink into my heart. I need faith to give you full access to my heart to allow you to do amazing things in my life. Show me how to conquer my doubt, Lord. Help me to rely on you instead of the things that have become a crutch in my life.

_____

_____

_____

_____

Lord, you are the source of goodness, so everything you do is good. Help me to think of you not in terms of human limitations, but instead in terms of your unmatched power and love. In the name of Jesus, I pray. Amen.

6
From Devastation to Transformation

Most of us never intended to be in the situations we find ourselves in. We didn't intend for our children to be raised in a home without two loving parents. We didn't plan to find ourselves without a partner to walk through life with.

And if we're putting it all out there, sometimes it feels like "happily ever after" has turned into "happy never after." *Amlright?!*

But God uses all the junk in our lives for our good, when we put our trust in Him. I know it's hard to understand sometimes why God would allow us to go through so much pain. Raise your hand if you've ever said, "Okay God, feel free to rescue me at any time!"

But God uses hard times to *transform* us, to make us into something unique and new. He doesn't want to leave us like we are. He desires to change us into the gorgeous creation He intended for us to be all along.

Take heart, sister– you're not the first person to ever wonder, "Why does it have to be this hard though?" We may not fully understand God's methods, but in Isaiah 55:9, God says, "For just as the heavens are higher than the earth, so my ways are higher than your ways and my thoughts are higher than your thoughts."

And we're not just talking a little higher. Like infinitely higher. Infinitely better.

The messes of our lives are no match for God. Out of the utter wreckage of your pain, He can masterfully refashion you into the emboldened and unbound woman He designed you to be. The pain and limitations of our human experience eventually give way to reveal God's intricate workmanship in our lives. And while the process can be hard to comprehend, at the end of our understanding is the place where the most profound encounters with God take place, as we surrender our lives to let Him do what we could never do for ourselves.

Yes, I know it is painful. But how glorious the transformation will be.

In this section, you will see Jesus's perspective on human weakness and the good that can come from it. You will also look at the role of choices in the process of transformation, and the significance of taking action in faith.

PROBLEM

How have you felt circumstances, whether past or present, have limited or hindered you? Are you where you thought you would be in life? Why or why not?

PASSAGE

> 1 As Jesus was walking along, he saw a man who had been blind from birth. 2 "Rabbi," his disciples asked him, "why was this man born blind? Was it because of his own sins or his parents' sins?"
>
> 3 "It was not because of his sins or his parents' sins," Jesus answered. "This happened so the power of God could be seen in him. 4 We must quickly carry out the tasks assigned us by the one who sent us. The night is coming, and then no one can work. 5 But while I am here in the world, I am the light of the world."
>
> 6 Then he spit on the ground, made mud with the saliva, and spread the mud over the blind man's eyes. 7 He told him, "Go wash yourself in the pool of Siloam" (Siloam means "sent"). So the man went and washed and came back seeing!
>
> 8 His neighbors and others who knew him as a blind beggar asked each other, "Isn't this the man who used to sit and beg?" 9 Some said he was, and others said, "No, he just looks like him!" But the beggar kept saying, "Yes, I am the same one!"
>
> 10 They asked, "Who healed you? What happened?" 11 He told them, "The man they call Jesus made mud and spread it over my eyes and told me, 'Go to the pool of Siloam and wash yourself.' So I went and washed, and now I can see!"
>
> John 9:1-11

PROMISES

How long does verse 1 say the blind man had been blind? Why did the disciples think he had been made blind?

Underline the reason Jesus stated the man was blind (verse 3). How is this different from the reasons the disciples speculated the man was blind?

This man's blindness had purpose! On the surface, this man appeared to have been afflicted by God as a punishment for sin. But Jesus reveals quite the opposite – in reality, this man had been hand- selected to serve as a beacon of God's glory.

How does this understanding of the reason for this man's blindness change your perspective of weakness?

Jesus talks more about living out the purpose we have been selected for in verses 4 and 5. Who does He say assigns tasks?

Circle the word in verse 4 that Jesus uses to show how we should respond to our God-ordained opportunities. Why does Jesus say we should work in this way?

Our lives are important to God, but we only have so much time to do what He has planned for us. In verse 7, where is the blind man told to wash? What does the name of this place mean?

Do you think the meaning of this place is significant?

Verse 7 also shows us that this man had to take action for his healing to be completed. What does this tell you about the role of choices and actions in your own healing journey?

What happened to the man after he washed? How do you think he felt? How do you think he felt about his former disability?

Verse 8 shows us what the man's life was like before he was healed. Did it change? Underline the words that support your answer.

How did the man's friends and neighbors react to the healing? What does this show you about how others may respond to your own transformation?

Who does the man born blind say was responsible for his healing? How does this relate to the reason Jesus stated he had been born blind back in verse 3?

What does this tell you about the potential within your own weakness and healing?

PLAN

What hardships, past and present, have made you feel rejected or unworthy?

How does the Passage show you God wants to use those hardships to bless you?

How could your healing and transformation bless those around you?

What thoughts are keeping you focused on hardships instead of the healing?

How does the way you talk about your struggles show where your focus is? Do you tend to look for explanations as to why something happened or solutions to the problem?

From this Passage, which do you think Jesus would have us focus on– explanations or solutions?

When it comes to dealing with your feelings, do you have a tendency to bottle up your feelings, or do you tend to share a lot?

As we've mentioned before, wise, godly women are essential to helping us communicate our feelings in healthy ways. If you are one who bottles things up, what are some strategies you might implement with your mentor to help you open up? Or if you tend to share a lot, how can your mentor help you avoid complaining so your conversations are focused on God's promises for your future instead?

PRAYER

Gracious Father, I am so thankful that you are both willing and able to heal my brokenness. Lord, your Word says that you desire to not only restore me but transform me into a beautiful reflection of you. Lord, I am thankful that you have supreme power over my weaknesses and my circumstances, and that you use them to bring good things to me. Father, sometimes it is hard to see what you are doing. There are things that are hurting me, that I want to turn over to you because only you can make something good from it all.

_____

_____

_____

_____

Help me to know and trust that you see my pain, Lord. Strengthen my faith so I will not get tired and give up, but instead press on to see the beautiful things you will create from it all. In the name of Jesus, I pray. Amen.

7
Triumph Through Tears: When Grief Gives Way

As a single woman, you have suffered loss, in one form or another. Death, abandonment, betrayal– one or more of these has left you without the person you may have believed would walk through life with you. As you already know, the experience of going from "coupled" to "single" is full of grief.

Because, if you really look at it– something has died.

It's the grieving process of uncoupling that often makes us feel like we are losing our minds. One day, we're doing okay. The next day, we're weeping in a pile of old photos on the floor. Just when the pain appears to be subsiding, we get blind-sighted by some Hallmark movie moment that leaves us feeling a pain deeper than we've known before.

It. Is. Exhausting.

Psalm 34:18 says "The LORD is close to the brokenhearted; he rescues those whose spirits are crushed." In our grief, the Lord is close. In Psalm 56:8, David says that God, "keep[s] track of all [our] sorrows. [He has] collected all [our] tears in [His] bottle. [He has] recorded each one in [His] book."

A bottle of *your* tears. A book of *your* sorrows. Now that's profound.

The heartbreak you have longed to forget, God doesn't just see– He remembers, in painstaking detail. With tender concern, He desires to rescue you from your sorrow. But, as with many things God wants to do for us, we have to let Him.

And that means letting go.

We have to let go of what we thought life would be like. Let go of the dreams that have died. Let go of the future that will never be.

But in place of what was lost, God promises to do something completely new. The first step is finding our comfort in Him, and trusting Him to write the next chapter.

And girl, I promise you– it's better than a Hallmark movie.

In this section, you will understand more about the process of grief and what it can bring about in your life. You'll also discover the source of true joy, a joy that overcomes all circumstances.

PROBLEM

As a single mother, how have you struggled with feelings of loss and sorrow?

PASSAGE

> 20 I tell you the truth, you will weep and mourn over what is going to happen to me, but the world will rejoice. You will grieve, but your grief will suddenly turn to wonderful joy. 21 It will be like a woman suffering the pains of labor. When her child is born, her anguish gives way to joy because she has brought a new baby into the world. 22 So you have sorrow now, but I will see you again; then you will rejoice, and no one can rob you of that joy.
>
> John 16:20-22

PROMISES

In this passage, Jesus is preparing His followers for what they will experience when He is crucified. Circle the words in verse 20 that describe what Jesus says they will do and feel. How do these words relate to your own feelings of loss?

Underline what Jesus says in verse 20 the disciples' grief will turn into. Though the suffering itself may take time, what word does Jesus use to describe the manner in which the change will come about when it finally occurs?

What life experience does Jesus compare grieving to in verse 21?

How does your own experience with childbirth help you understand the metaphor Jesus uses?

In verse 21, underline what Jesus says a woman experiences when her child is finally born. Why does He say this happens?

What does the new baby represent in this metaphor?

> Childbirth is a process, and so is grief. And just as the pain of labor yields to the joy of birth, eventually the suffering of grief also gives way to new life.

What comfort can understanding this provide you when you think of your own grief and loss?

In verse 22, what promises does Jesus offer the disciples?

Jesus helps the disciples see beyond their present suffering with promises of a bright future. How can you embrace these same promises in your own grieving process?

Underline what Jesus says about the joy the disciples will experience. What other words would you use to characterize this kind of joy?

What is the source of this joy Jesus promises? What does this teach you about the source of a joy that defies the circumstances of your own life?

PLAN

How does the Passage connect with your own feelings of grief and loss?

Does this Passage enhance your understanding of the grieving process?

Jesus compared grief to labor. How does the metaphor of childbirth help you understand the time grieving takes?

Have you tried to hurry your own grieving process along?

How do you think your children are experiencing loss? Does your understanding of grief give you any insights into their behavior?

The good news is we don't have to wait for suffering to end before we can experience the kind of joy Jesus promises. While the circumstances of life change, God never changes, and that is something to rejoice in. What would it look like for you to rejoice in your sorrow?

Rejoicing takes many forms– while we often think of singing, praising, or dancing, identifying our God-given abilities and enjoying these blessings is another form of rejoicing. What unique talents and interests has God blessed you with? Consider things like playing music, writing, crafting, cooking, serving, or exercising.

How can you use these abilities or interests this week as an act of worship?

How can you encourage your children to use their own gifts in a similar way?

Loving God, you see the grief I am enduring. You see the pain my children are experiencing. I am thankful that Jesus didn't just come to Earth to tell us about suffering; He experienced it on my behalf so that I would be comforted and healed. Lord, seeking comfort in my sorrow tempts me to turn to things other than you to cope with the pain. Your Word tells me these things won't last because you are the source of true joy. I want to turn to you instead and kick the habits that are keeping me from experiencing real peace in this time of sadness.

_____

_____

_____

_____

Help me to know this suffering is temporary, just like the anguish of childbirth. You will bring forth new life from this pain, but I am hurting while I wait, Lord. Help me to know that you won't leave me like this, and that by the power of the Holy Spirit, I can overcome. In Jesus's name, I pray. Amen.

8
All Things New: God's Perfect Plan for Your Future

At this point in your life, I know you've seen your dreams die right in front of you. And even if you've managed to surrender them to God and leave them behind, if you're like me, you're probably wondering how you're going to keep your new dreams from suffering the same fate as your old ones.

Thankfully, God is SO much better at the "new dreams" thing than we ever could be. James 1:17 (ESV) says "every good gift and every perfect gift is from above."

Read that again. Every. Perfect. Gift.

And better still, *God doesn't give gifts like we give* (cue Christmas shopping stress). Jesus told His followers in Matthew 7:11, "if you sinful people know how to give good gifts to your children, how much more will your heavenly Father give good gifts to those who ask Him."

To those who ask Him. With God, we don't have to hold back. He invites us to ask! God is in the business of new things, sister. And He is eager to give new dreams, and a new life, to you.

And one more thing. As you run ahead into His glorious future, don't let the old stuff trip you up (cuz you know it will try to grab you by the ankles like a needy toddler). Old habits. Old fears. Old comforts. When you are at your lowest, your old life and your old dreams will seem like that ratty, faded sweatshirt we all have in the back of the closet– familiar and easy.

But don't fall for it, friend. It's a trap.

When we are at our weakest, we're often tempted to trade the promises of an uncertain future for a life that seems to be oh-so-comfortable (for now). But instead of giving in to that way of thinking, do what Ephesians 4:22-24 (ESV) encourages all of us to do: "Put off your old self, which belongs to your former manner of life" and "put on the new self, created after the likeness of God."

When you consciously, consistently <u>choose your future</u> over your past, you both declare Christ's victory over your past life *and* claim the inheritance of a new future as a rightful daughter of The King. It's not always easy, but it's so, so worth it.

So keep putting on that new self, girl. That *free* self. That *worthy* self. That *beloved* self. That *victorious* self. Wear it proudly like the glorious crown of jewels it is. And don't let that ratty-old-sweatshirt of a life come back to take away your new, fabulous future in Christ.

In this section, you will read about God's excitement for what He has planned for the future. You will also see how He is the God who takes action, even when we aren't aware that He's doing anything.

PROBLEM

What fears do you have about your future?

PASSAGE

> 16 I am the LORD, who opened a way through the waters,
> making a dry path through the sea.
> 17 I called forth the mighty army of Egypt
> with all its chariots and horses.
> I drew them beneath the waves, and they drowned,
> their lives snuffed out like a smoldering candlewick.
> 18 "But forget all that—
> it is nothing compared to what I am going to do.
> 19 For I am about to do something new.
> See, I have already begun! Do you not see it?
> I will make a pathway through the wilderness.
> I will create rivers in the dry wasteland.
> 20 The wild animals in the fields will thank me,
> the jackals and owls, too,
> for giving them water in the desert.
> Yes, I will make rivers in the dry wasteland
> so my chosen people can be refreshed.
>
> Isaiah 43:16-20

PROMISES

What biblical event is referenced in verses 16-17?

The Exodus occurred hundreds of years prior to this prophecy being recorded by Isaiah – the Israelites being addressed in this Passage were centuries removed from the actual event itself. Why do you think God, through the prophet Isaiah, recounts this event in this Passage?

What does reminding these Israelites of the Exodus demonstrate to them about God's power and care for His people?

Underline what God says in verse 18 the Israelites should do with that memory of the Exodus. What is the reason He says to do that?

What does this show us about the perspective we should have on the past– even the good parts– compared to God's future plans?

Underline what God says in verse 19 He is about to do. Underline the word that shows when God will begin. What does this show you about our awareness of God's workings in our lives?

> God doesn't wait for us to be aware of what He is doing before He acts- He is always at work, whether we know it or not.

Underline the action words in verses 19 and 20 that show what God says He is going to do. What does the first sentence of verse 20 say the recipients of His work will do in response?

Can these recipients provide for themselves? When you consider what God promises to provide them, what about their location is significant?

What does the recipients' inability to provide for themselves show you about God's awareness and compassion?

What does this indicate to you about God's consideration of your own needs, whether physical, emotional, or spiritual?

Underline the word in verse 20 that shows God's specific purpose for bringing "rivers in the dry wasteland." How does this word make you feel when you consider that God wants to do new things in and for you too?

What did God do with water back in verse 17? How does this differ from the way He intends to use water in verse 20?

God is infinitely creative, and we shouldn't limit our belief in what God can do by thinking the future will look exactly like the past.

What does this passage reveal to you about God's nature?

PLAN

How often do you find yourself comparing your current circumstances to your past?

How often do you feel doubtful or hopeless about the future?

How are memories of the past, or ruined dreams of your future, causing you pain?

What triggers these thoughts?

What do you think it would feel like to "put on your new self" and walk in Christ's victory over your life?

Remembering what God has done in the past reminds us of God's love and compassion towards us, despite our present circumstances. What has God done for you in the past to demonstrate His care for you?

Gratitude also helps us stay focused on what God is doing, rather than getting bogged down by stress and pain. What do you see that God is doing in your life now? In your kids' lives?

Praise is SO powerful. The Bible tells us that praise is a weapon that protects us and brings forth God's mighty vengeance over anything that tries to oppose us (Psalm 149). This week, how can you emphasize praising God for what He has done, and what He is doing?

How can you involve your children?

PRAYER

Mighty Father, you are the God of new things. You are the God of promises. I am thankful you don't give blessings to us in limited human ways but in limitlessly generous and creative ways. Sometimes I am afraid of what my future holds. Sometimes I don't see how my future could be any better than the life that is now behind me. But your Word reminds me that all of your gifts are perfect. You know what is good for me, and you want me to have it. Help me to trust that when I follow you, I will see that what you have for me is exactly what I need. Help me not to wait in anxiety, but to walk in that trust today. Turn my attention to the good you are already doing in my life, that I grow in praise and gratitude for all you are.

_____

_____

_____

_____

God, you see my broken dreams. Thank you for showing me that you have new dreams for me. Teach me to be patient as these new dreams unfold in your perfect timing. In the name of Jesus, I pray. Amen.

NOTES

ABOUT THE AUTHOR

Michelle Donnelly is the mother of three precious children, two girls and a boy. Through a tumultuous marriage and divorce, God brought profound healing to Michelle and her children. Over time, God revealed to Michelle that her pain would give way to purpose. She launched Agape Moms, an outreach that ministers to single mothers. Michelle's passion is to see single mothers set free from the bondage of their suffering, to walk in the victory and joy of Jesus Christ, through the power of the Holy Spirit.

Michelle holds a Master's degree in Leadership from Grand Canyon University in Phoenix, Arizona. She and her family live near Nashville, where they enjoy impromptu pancake breakfasts, summertime creek walks, and incredibly corny jokes.

ABOUT AGAPE MOMS

Agape Moms is an outreach dedicated to encouraging single mothers through the unconditional 'agape' love of Jesus Christ.

Join our community! Receive helpful tips from our blog, access ministry tools for your own outreach to single mothers, and download free wallpapers at www.agapemoms.com

Connect with us on Facebook and Instagram @agapemoms

Made in the
USA
Lexington, KY